D1368700

LUDION PUBLISHER

The First Decade!

**DESIGNERS
AGAINST AIDS**

INTRO

I gladly accepted to write the introduction to this book because I admire the positive spirit and unique vision of Ninette Murk. Ninette is a pioneer in her own way, by using art and pop culture to increase global awareness of AIDS among young people.

About 10 years ago, Ninette worked as a freelance fashion editor. Back then, she lost her best friend to AIDS and decided to turn a dramatic story into a positive one. As a single mother of two children she took up a huge challenge and launched a unique idea: Designers Against Aids.

The very first DAA projects were small in scale and were located in Antwerp, the city of fashion. Very soon however, DAA attracted the interest of big international names such as Yoko Ono, Dita Von Teese, Estelle, Tokio Hotel and Robert Smith, who got involved because they connected both to the cause and the project. Even France's First Lady Carla Bruni Sarkozy – as Ambassador for The Global Fund to fight AIDS, TB and malaria – recently wrote a letter in which she expressed her admiration for the good work delivered by DAA.

Today, DAA is creating global awareness not only through fashion, but also via all sorts of pop art expressions such as the fantastic pictures you will see in this book. DAA has indeed grown into a unique international story. Many companies have shown great interest in the project and are getting involved through their corporate responsibility programs. The Public Private Partnership between DAA and the Swedish fashion company H&M for instance, going into its 4th year in 2012, sets a perfect example for other companies around the world to care about the subject and to financially support organizations such as DAA.

I hope that through this book, even more people will get to know the wonderful work of DAA. I trust that this book will bring along new opportunities to further increase awareness among young people. Indeed, AIDS is not over by any means and the world can't afford to ignore this threat. Over 7 000 people get infected with HIV every day and 5 500 people die every day. We must redouble our efforts to stop this terrible epidemic.

I wish there were more people like Ninette. The world would be a better place.

Professor Peter Piot
Director, London School of Hygiene & Tropical Medicine
Former Executive Director of UNAIDS

BEAUTY WITHOUT IRONY

"NINETTE MURK"

When was the last time your breath was taken away by some amazing sight or sound? When you felt gooseflesh creeping all the way up your arms and tears filling your eyes just because something was so unbeliev- ably beautiful? And after that, what happened? Could you admit the feeling to yourself and – heaven forbid – to others as well? Without cracking jokes about getting old and sentimental? Good. Because honest appreciation of all things beautiful is the way forward.

While researching this story I talked to a lot of people – fashion professionals and others – about the subject and all, with the exception of one – who understood 'beauty without ironing' (!) – knew exactly what I was on about and agreed with me fully: it's very relaxing to finally drop that cool front and admit you love seeing fine paintings, haute couture and ballet, you like to listen to classical music once in a while – harmonic melodies are easy on the ears after all – and even romantic sunsets, newborn puppies and other so-called clichés have a certain appeal. They're not clichés for nothing, right?

Enjoying beauty is firstly a very physical experience, almost scarily so. Remember sitting on a football terrace with loads of enthousiastic fans, or being present at the singing of the national hymn – you, as a cool person, of course kept your lips firmly sealed – and you couldn't help but feeling moved by the singing masses? Admit it and it feels even better. All that gooseflesh and those dilated pupils, rapid heartbeats and deep breathing must be good for something.

Before you all rush out now and become nationalistic hooligans (don't believe the hype, you fools!), what I'd really like to plead for is a more private joy of beauty, one to be found in abundance in the arts, fashion and music. More and more so in fact. I mean, how far can you go with destruction? Decibels? Irony? Or the mother of all cowards, sarcasm? Let's all just sit at home or in a 'trendy' bar dressed in our 'ironic' trashed & customized outfits and complain, shall we? That'll teach the world a thing or two. Except, I don't think so.

With a little help from my friends... Of course there's more to this renewed interest in – and appreciation for – beauty than just nice clothes, paintings and music: it's a general feeling among people of wanting to help each other out as much as possible, of friendship, support and admiration for each other's work and efforts. While big conglomerates thrive on competition and one-upmanship, young designers and other creatives like photographers, stylists, graphic designers and DJ's form small groups that are forever changing and networking (read: partying) in an informal way, having fun, doing their own thing and getting noticed in the process. No pushiness, no hypes, no competition, no big dreams of ruling the world (OK, maybe secretly at night, when no-one's looking), just wanting to create something that's unique, honest, instinctive and – here it comes again – beautiful. In the eye of the beholder. Because together with this new appreciation of beauty also comes a new definition of what beauty really is. Symmetry, as science tried to teach us for decades? Humbug. Give us imperfection and gapped teeth any day. Gloss and perfection? Aaaaarrrrggghhhh! Who hasn't seen a grainy black & white photo of a big town backstreet and thought: now thàt's really beautiful? Without trying to be clever, just because you were touched by the image? Honesty, passion, creativity and humility – yeah, that old chestnut pops up again too – are what count and all I can hope is that this won't be a passing trend like so many others before. You may say that I'm a dreamer, but I surely am not the only one...

Go on, admit it, you really like beauty that way.

Feel better already?

THE MEANING OF DESIGN

"ALAIN DE BOTTON"

Is it serious to worry about design and architecture? To think hard about the shape of the bathroom taps, the colour of the bedspread and the dimensions of the window frames? A long intellectual tradition suggests it isn't quite. A whiff of trivia and self-indulgence floats over the topic. It seems like something best handled by the flamboyant presenters of early evening TV shows. A thought-provoking number of the world's most intelligent people have always disdained any interest in the appearance of buildings, equating contentment with discarnate and invisible matters instead. The Ancient Greek Stoic philosopher Epictetus is said to have demanded of a heart-broken friend whose house had burnt to the ground, 'If you really understand what governs the universe, how can you yearn for bits of stone and pretty rock?' (It is unclear how much longer the friendship lasted.)

And yet determined efforts to scorn design have also long been matched by equally persistent attempts to mould the material world to graceful ends. People have strained their backs carving flowers into their roof beams and their eyesight embroidering animals onto their tablecloths. They have given up weekends to hide unsightly cables behind ledges. They have thought carefully about appropriate kitchen work-surfaces. They have imagined living in unattainably expensive houses pictured in magazines and then felt sad, as one does on passing an attractive stranger in a crowded street.

We seem divided between an urge to override our senses and numb ourselves to the appearance of houses and a contradictory impulse to acknowledge the extent to which our identities are indelibly connected to, and will shift along with, our locations. I personally side with the view that it does (unfortunately as it's expensive) matter what things look like: an ugly room can coagulate any loose suspicions as to the incompleteness of life, while a sun-lit one set with honey-coloured limestone tiles can lend support to whatever is most hopeful within us. Belief in the significance of architecture is premised on the notion that we are, for better and for worse, different people in different places – and on the conviction that it is architecture's task to render vivid to us who we might ideally be.

Our sensitivity to our surroundings can be traced back to a troubling feature of human psychology: to the way we harbour within us many different selves, not all of which feel equally like 'us', so much so that in certain moods, we can complain of having come adrift from what we judge to be our true selves. Unfortunately, the self we miss at such moments, the elusively authentic, creative and spontaneous side of our character, is not ours to summon at will. Our access to it is, to a humbling extent, determined by the places we happen to be in, by the colour of the bricks, the height of the ceilings and the layout of the streets. In a house strangled by three motorways, or in a wasteland of rundown tower blocks, our optimism and sense of purpose are liable to drain away, like water from a punctured container. We may start to forget that we ever had ambitions or reasons to feel spirited and hopeful.

We depend on our surroundings obliquely to embody the moods and ideas we respect and then to remind us of them. We look to our buildings to hold us, like a kind of psychological mould, to a helpful vision of ourselves. We arrange around us material forms which communicate to us what we need – but are at constant risk of forgetting we need – within. We turn to wallpaper, benches, paintings and streets to staunch the disappearance of our true selves.

In turn, those places whose outlook matches and legitimates our own, we tend to honour with the term 'home'. Our homes do not have to offer us permanent occupancy or store our clothes to merit the name. To speak of home in relation to a building is simply to recognise its harmony with our own prized internal song. As the French writer Stendhal put it, 'What we find beautiful is the promise of happiness'.

It is the world's great religions that have perhaps given most thought to the role played by our environment in determining our identity and so – while seldom constructing places where we might fall asleep – have shown the greatest sympathy for our need for a home. The very principle of religious architecture has its origins in the notion that where we are critically determines what we are able to believe in. To defenders of religious architecture, however convinced we are at an intellectual level of our commitments to a creed, we will only remain reliably devoted to it when it is continually affirmed by our buildings. We may be nearer or further away from God on account of whether we're in a church, a mosque – or a supermarket. We can't be good, faithful people anywhere.
Ordinary, domestic architecture can be said to have just as much of an influence on our characters as religious buildings. What we call a beautiful house is one that rebalances our misshapen natures and encourages emotions which we are in danger of losing sight of. For example, an anxious person may be deeply moved by a white empty minimalist house. Or a business executive who spends her life shuttling between airports and steel and glass conference centres may feel an intense attraction to a simple rustic cottage – which can put her in

touch with sides of her personality that are denied to her in the ordinary press of her days. We call something beautiful whenever we detect that it contains in a concentrated form those qualities in which we personally, or our societies more generally, are deficient. We respect a style which can move us away from what we fear and towards what we crave: a style which carries the correct dosage of our missing virtues.

It is sometimes thought exaggerated to judge people on their tastes in design. It can hardly seem appropriate to pass judgement on the basis of a choice of wallpaper. But the more seriously we take architecture, the more we can come to argue that it is in fact logical to base a sympathy for someone on their visual tastes. For visual taste is never just simply a visual matter. It's indicative of a view of life. Any object of design will give off an impression of the psychological and moral attitudes it supports. We can, for example, feel two distinct conceptions of fulfilment emanating from a plain crockery set on the one hand and an ornate flower-encrusted one on the other – an invitation to a democratic graceful sensibility in the former case, to a more nostalgic, country-bound disposition in the latter.

In essence, what works of design and architecture talk to us about is the kind of life that would most appropriately unfold within and around them. They tell us of certain moods that they seek to encourage and sustain in their inhabitants. While keeping us warm and helping us in mechanical ways, they simultaneously hold out an invitation for us to be specific sorts of people. They speak of particular visions of happiness.
To describe a building as beautiful therefore suggests more than a mere aesthetic fondness; it implies an attraction to the particular way of life this structure is promoting through its roof, door handles, window frames, staircase and furnishings. A feeling of beauty is a sign that we have come upon a material articulation of certain of our ideas of a good life. Similarly, buildings will strike us as offensive not because they violate a private and mysterious visual preference but because they conflict with our understanding of the rightful sense of existence.

No wonder then that our discussions of architecture and design have a tendency to be so heated. Arguments about what is beautiful are at heart arguments about the values we want to live by – rather than merely struggles about how we want things to look.

Beauty
Holy

Without

Daniel Riera

Erwin Olaf

Teun Voeten

Jimmy Kets

IMAGINA A PAZ

رویای صلح **IMMAGINA LA PACE** חלום שלום

ཞི་བ་སྒོམས། წარმოიდგინეთ მშვიდობა

BARIŞI DÜŞLE **ILARAWAN ANG MUNDONG MAPAYAPA**

평화를 꿈꾸자 **IMAGINA LA PAZ**

ᓴᐃᒪᕐᑲᑎᒌᑦᑕ **IMAGINE PEACE** احلم سلام

KUVITTELE RAUHA 想像世界有了和平

STELL DIR VOR ES IST FRIEDEN **HUGSA SÉR FRIÐ**

TUFIKIRIENI AMANI **KÉPZELD EL A BÉKÉT**

IMAGINEZ LA PAIX சமாதானத்தை நினையுங்கள்

ПРЕДСТАВЬТЕ СЕБЕ МИР शान्ति की कल्पना करें

平和な世界を想像してごらん

love, yoko

Pat Kurs

Zoltan Gerliczki

Ronald Van der Hilst

Douglas Friedman

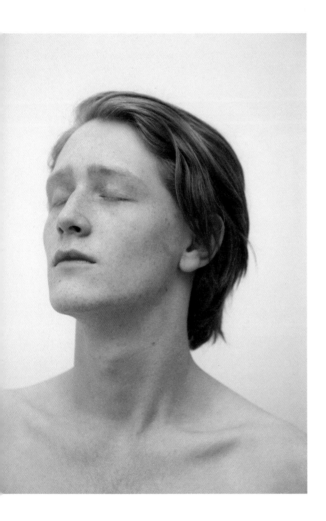

Eva Gödel

Nick Hannes

Sarah Van Marcke

Diane Pernet

Jef Paepen

Layla Aerts

Karim Rashid

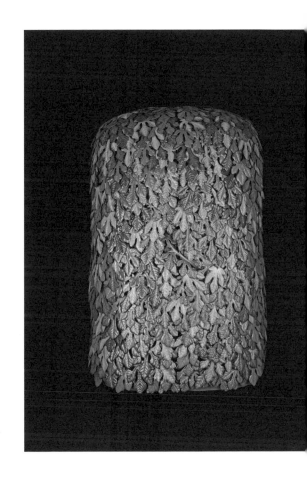

Tord Boontje

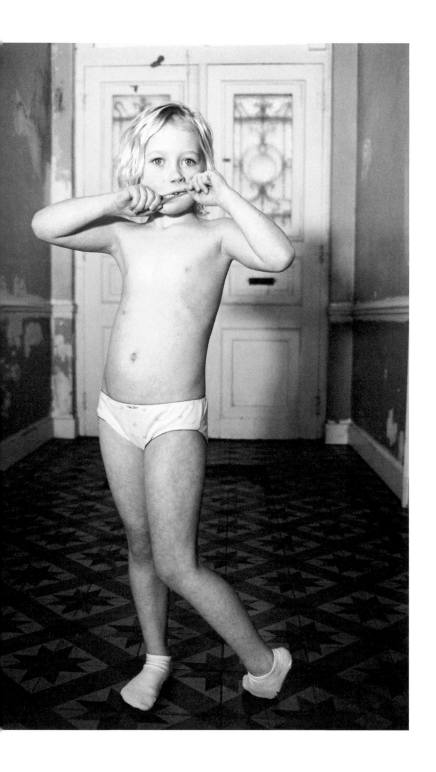

Elke Boon

Sandrine Dulermo & Michael Labica

1

2

3

Martin Bing

Vincent W. Gagliostro

Dominik Gigler

Mick Traen

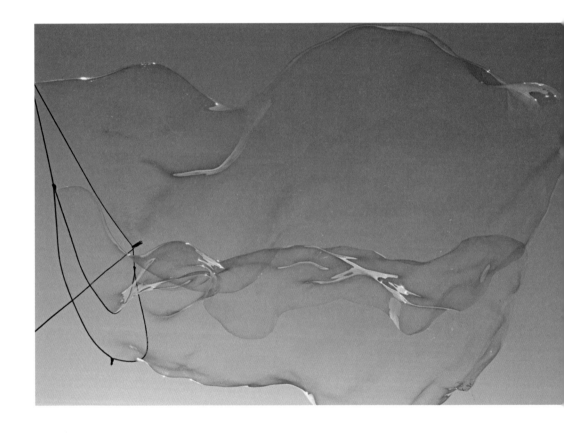

Lars Stephan

Frank Horvat

Gianluca Tamorri

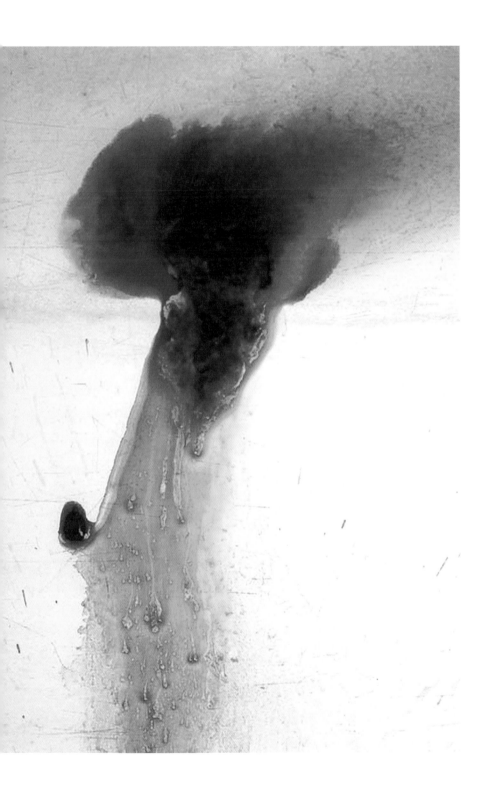

Sara Claes

PETIT MORCE
DE CIEL EN
FORME DE
DÉSIR

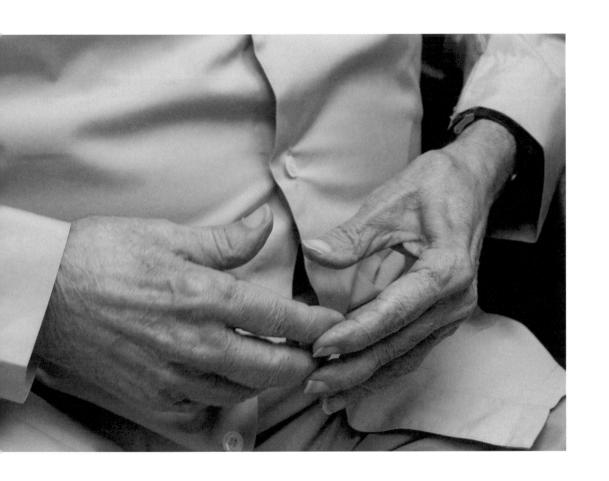

Romulo Fialdinini

Dirk Swartenbroekx

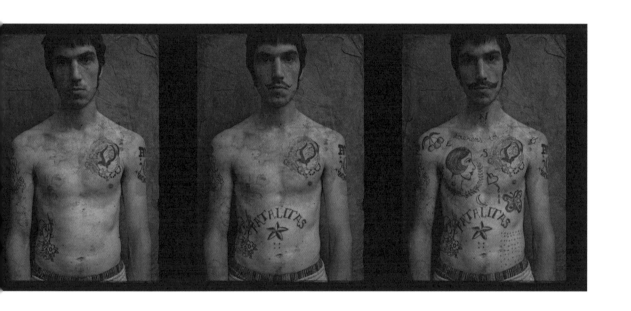

Valérie Servant

Hannelore Knuts

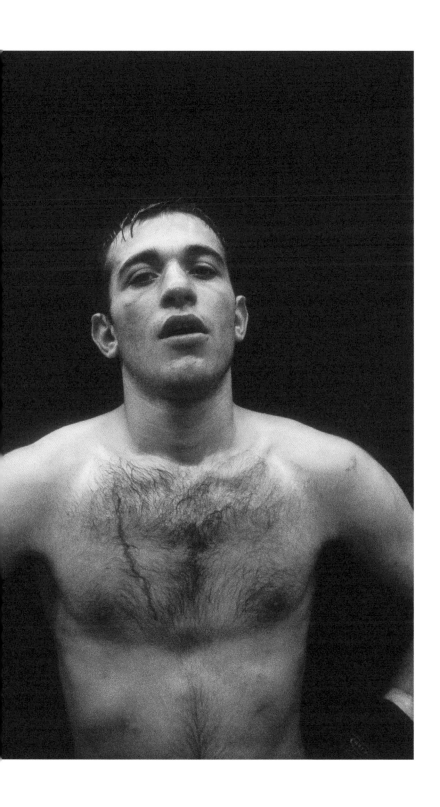

Franky Claeys

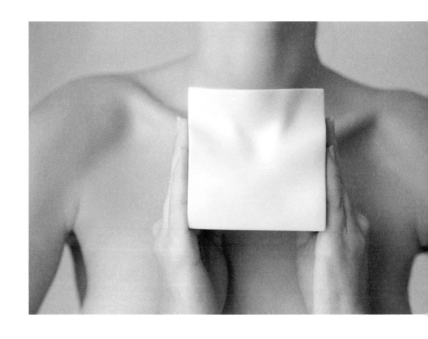

Ike Udé

TIM VAN STEENBERGEN
MITZLAVV BVBA
HERENTALSEBAAN 56-58
2100 DEURNE (ANTWERP)
BELGIUM
(www.timvansteenbergen.com)
+ stones swarovski
Toppart
FRONT
OFFICE: MITZLAVV BVBA
TEL: +32 3 237 87 00 | FAX: +32 3 237 04 70 | mail@timvansteenbergen.com
VAT BE 0475 787 869 (RPR Antwerpen) | ACCOUNT 320-0063839-83 | IBAN BE14 3200 0638 3983 | BIC BBRUBE
Tim Van Steenbergen is a registered trademark licensed to Mitzlavv BVBA

Jason (Woei-Ping) Chen

Filip Van Roe

Riitta Päiväläinen

Elisabeth Novick

Diego Franssens

Xander Ferreira

Dominic Sio

Franky Verdickt

Chris Plytas

Ben Van Alboom

IN THE DAYS TO COME ALL WILL BE FORGOTTEN

Mark Titchner

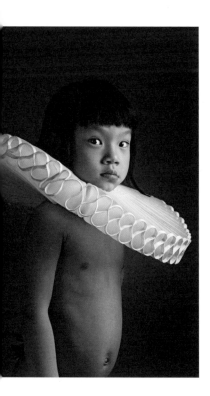

Filip Naudts

Piet Raemdonck

Thomas Vanhaute

Luiz Carlos Barreto

Tom and Bill Kaulitz

Jamie Brennan

Tom Tosseyn

Ali Mahdavi

Antonio Paladino

Jean Claude Wouters

Peggy Sirota

ADIOS
PARADISE

Andy Wauman

Annelies De Mey

Thierry Van Biesen

Sophie Rata

Vera Valdez

Daniel Jackson

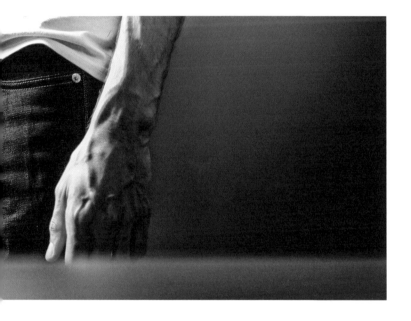

Marc Atlan

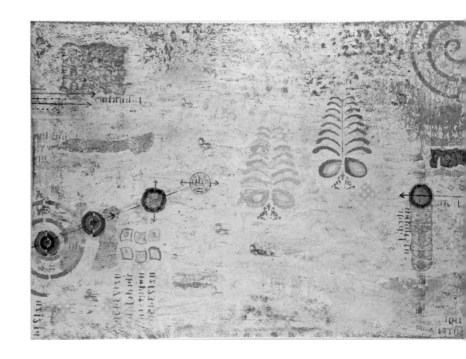

Monika Macken

Ole Stragier

Glenn Glasser

Candice Mai Khanh Nguyen

Tinko Czetwertynski

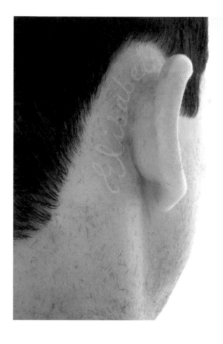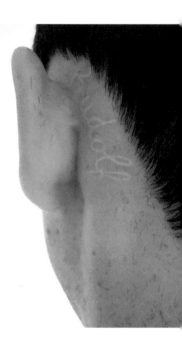

Jordan Betten

Jürgen Nefzger

Michel Vaerewijck

Eva Vermandel

Joss McKinley

Annick Geenen

Karin Hanssen

Ellie Van Den Brande

Tom and Bill Kaulitz

Wayne Hemingway

Jessica Antola

Bert Danckaert

Titus Simoens

Werner Van Reck

Deborah Irmas

Danny Veys

Kimiko Yoshida

Javier Barcala

Nadine Tasseel

Frances Joossens

Piet Goethals

Valéry Grancher

Jamie Campbell

Vera Lehndorf & Andreas Hubertus Ilse

LOVE IS MY RELIGION

"NINETTE MURK"

Paris, October 17, 1993. After our invitations had been checked with the gravity and thoroughness you would expect from the security service of a particularly paranoid president, we entered the stately 19th century building and were immediately immersed in a vaguely malicious hubbub. It was caused by a mixture of journalists, style prophets and other self-proclaimed VIPs who were exchanging dishonest pleasantries while glancing around for an opportunity to socialize with someone even higher on the pecking order. At a fashion show – because that's what it was – hierarchy is crucial, you see. The really important people get front row seats and from there it goes all the way to the back of the venue, to the standing places where the up & coming (and a few down & almost out) reside; the way your status is established and by whom is a mystery that closely resembles alchemy. At any rate, I was both pleased and annoyed to see that I was entitled to a seat. Pleased, because after suffering a intracranial haemorrhage some time before, I found it hard to stand up for a long period of time. Of course I also couldn't help but think "wow, I'm about to rub shoulders with the fashion editor of a pretty good newspaper and a one hit wonder whose song terrorised the charts last year. Not bad for a freelance hack who's only been at it for a few years." It not only showed that I had somehow forgotten my pledge to smother this particular songwriter in the filthiest sewer around, it also meant that I was slowly turning from lead to gold and I couldn't help but feel a pang of pride about that. Oh vanities... Unfortunately it also meant that my friend and colleague Peter wouldn't be sitting next to me because, needless to say, lowly stylists aren't accorded the same privileges. He was relegated to the standing places. While waiting for the show to start, I was wondering what the hell I was doing in a place like this anyway – a thought that had been occurring to me disturbingly often for some time – when there was a commotion behind me. Noticing that Peter was somehow involved I made my way to the back. It turned out he had had the audacity to bring a small folding chair. Peter was arguing fiercely with the fashion designer's PR girl and two ushers, whose usual disdain was now replaced by apoplectic rage and utter disbelief. A folding chair! Unbelievable!

What's the point of giving someone a standing place only for him to bring his own chair? Clearly, the world must soon come to an end if they were going to allow such insolence.

Peter was fast running out of steam and that was exactly why he had brought the chair. I joined the fray and explained to the clipboard Nazis that Peter had a very good reason for doing what he did: he was HIV-positive and got tired very quickly. Without blinking, the PR woman replied: "If he's ill, he shouldn't come to a fashion show. He only causes trouble." We left without saying another word.

Four months after this happened, Peter Verhelst died from AIDS-related complications.

THANK YOU! ACKNOW-LEDGE-MENTS

Every now and then, people have told me that I should write a book about my life. I always laughed it off saying that a) I couldn't see the point and b) I was fairly confident that, at the launch party, they would be toasting the success of a very slim volume indeed. Ludion's Christoph Ruys happily ignored my objections and approached me in the spring of 2010 with the proposal to publish a book about the first decade of Designers against AIDS, including related HIV/AIDS projects and – last but not least – the art collective that I'm proud to coordinate, Beauty without Irony. He hastened to add a promise that part of the sales proceeds would go to the new DAA education center and that the book would be about my work, not my life. In the end I agreed mainly because DAA needs all the money and publicity that it can get. While I was working my way through ten years' worth of archives, photo albums, cardboard boxes full of clothing and a ridiculous amount of digital stuff to compile material for the book, my personal life started to pop up at all-too-frequent intervals. I soon realised that it was going to be impossible to keep the last part of that promise, if the book was going to have any affinity with reality. The thing is that I tend to mix work and my private life to such an extent that it drives those who are close to me crazy.

My first thanks therefore goes to my husband Peke, without whose support a lot of my projects wouldn't have worked out the way they did and whose love is wrapped around me like a cashmere blanket. And to my children Mischa and Nona. I guess they'd have loved to hear me talk about other stuff than work, events and projects sometimes, but that didn't happen very often when they were young. God knows how they managed to turn out to be such fantastic adults with such a workaholic for a mother, but they did. And hooray for that.

Someone else who has been sailing with me on the choppy seas of my projects, dreams and illusions is Javier Barcala. He was the creative director of DAA from 2004 until 2009 and became a close friend and ally over the years. Sometimes, things didn't go as smoothly as we would have liked to, but all those amazing moments we shared together easily made up for that (remember those crocodiles and the boat tour in the Florida Keys during the Fashion against AIDS shoot in Miami?). Javier played a crucial role in helping to develop Designers against AIDS to become a globally appreciated non-profit organisation with a safe sex message that reaches young people via pop culture. Gracias por todo!

Many thanks also to Jan Nord and Jorgen Andersson at H&M in Stockholm, who saw the potential of a Public Private Partnership between H&M and DAA as early as 2006, long before anybody else. Thanks to their donations – the result of three Fashion against AIDS collections – we have now been able to establish our first International HIV/AIDS Awareness Education Center in Belgium. Hopefully, more centers will follow.

At this point I must mention Peter Verhelst (1964-1994) who played an important, but all too brief part in our story. He was a young Belgian fashion stylist and a dear friend of mine. After his studies at the Antwerp Fashion Academy he worked as an assistant to fashion editor Gerdi Esch for women's weekly Flair and then joined me at the newspaper Het Volk, where he took over from me as their fashion editor as I left to focus on a freelance career. Peter was one of the first people I knew who was very open about being HIV-positive, which was not an obvious thing to do in those days. He also – albeit probably unwittingly – showed me the way forward. I miss you so much, Peter... You made it all happen.

I would also like to heap gratitude upon everyone who was in any way involved in getting this book published: Michael James O'Brien, Zoltan Gerliczki, Steffi Tisson, Bess Stonehouse, Candice Nguyen, Tinneke Janssens, Sandra Deakin, Christoph Ruys, Gunther De Wit, BASEdesign and Anne Davis. Of course I apologize to all those whom I am bound to have forgotten, including everyone who has, at some point, selflessly helped me in my endeavours over the years.

Finally, I would like to thank all the artists, designers, musicians, journalists, photographers, printers, architects, companies and organizations who have supported my work and who helped some important dreams become true, especially my hero professor Peter Piot, who kindly agreed to write the foreword of this book.

This is only the beginning – nobody knows what the next decade will bring, but we'll be going forward no matter what happens. It's the only way to go.

Ninette Murk, August 2010

CHAPTER ONE

After the incident in Paris, I continued to work as a fashion journalist but my initial feelings of discomfort only became stronger as the old millennium made way for the new one. At some point I realised I was actually starting to hate certain aspects of the industry and all that orbits it. It was hard not to feel like a hypocrite. I didn't want to be part of it yet I kept on writing about it, fully aware of the fact that every article I wrote was promoting not only the creative geniuses that I admired, but also the negative aspects.

Mind you, I loved most parts of my job. I loved the creativity of designers and the way they constantly challenge both themselves and the public with new concepts and ideas. I loved the energy, the surprises, the close friendships, the wackiness of it all. It's the main reason why I did what I did. But surely, there must be another way to enjoy those benefits and to work with creative people? To do something positive, rather than just documenting an industry which is basically nihilistic. Make the world a better place perhaps? A better place in which I would still get paid of course. Because let's be honest – hello again fashion industry! – money does make the world go round. It even turns an old hippie into a fashion journalist.

After my divorce, I ended up as a single mom with two children to raise. Not having had any formal schooling to speak of I couldn't find a job so I had to fall back on unemployment benefits and welfare. I soon started thinking about my options. Clearly, making ends meet on child support and government hand-outs was a dead-end street (a dark, unsavoury alley in fact) but what else could I possibly do? I really had no idea. To pass the time, I wrote the occasional column for my friends' reading pleasure and at some point one of them said my musings were quite funny and well written. Maybe I could "do something" with that? The guy – being a chronically drunk singer – had absolutely no idea as to how or where, but I liked the idea – if only because I couldn't come up with anything else. Eventually I got a position with a local theatre magazine, through my children's babysitter of all people. It was unpaid and the paper had a circulation of about 12. Nonetheless, it was a start and before long I got a real job (with real money, I was amazed to discover) at a woman's monthly and things took off from there. Some time later, I became self-employed and made fashion my speciality. I started to work for a number of magazines and newspapers both in Belgium and abroad, including a few pretty prestigious ones. Much to her own surprise, Ninette Murk became a known quantity in the field. I'd like to say it was all due to hard work and me being incredibly talented, but obviously a considerable amount of luck (as in meeting the right people at the right time) was involved too. In the process, I also met and became friends with a lot of fashion designers and other artists from all walks of life. If something made my job as a journalist worthwhile in the long run, then it surely must be getting to know all those wonderful – albeit often somewhat eccentric – people. I also got to know and had to work with individuals and institutions whose ethics and outlook didn't appeal to me at all. Which brings us neatly to 2001.

In June of that year, Serkan Sarier graduated at the top of his class of the Antwerp Fashion Academy (or whatever they're it calling today – it changes names faster than Elvis Pompilio switches hats) and of course I attended the graduation show. I had absolutely no idea that it was going to be a pivotal moment in my life. On the contrary, as student after student herded his models over the catwalk I gloomily started to conclude that the evening was going to be a waste of time; it was all fairly dull, depressing and uninspiring. Until Serkan's part of the show – the very last one – started. Using ballerinas and music by Shostakovich, he created a moment of total and uncompromising beauty. I almost fell off my front row seat. I may have used the phrase "blown away" a bit too often in my articles before, but this time it was fully justified. I was in awe and couldn't help but think "This is so very real. So true. This is beauty without any irony whatsoever." It was a moment of complete awareness. Suddenly I knew what to do, what I wanted to support with all my heart and soul. The proverbial thunderbolt had struck.

CHAPTER TWO

I would like to say that the days after my eureka moment were spent in quiet contemplation but that would be a blatant lie. I'm the sort of person who, once fired up, rushes headlong into things and the distinct possibility of detours and the need to backtrack a bit won't keep me from trying everything first. Impulses rule! So I set to work straight away. This may not seem like an easy task when all you have is a very vague idea and the phrase "beauty without irony" but it was as if a dam had burst. The ideas came in such rapid succession that I still find it difficult to believe it ever happened. I can't even remember writing the BWI manifesto:

"When was the last time your breath was taken away by some amazing sight or sound? That you felt gooseflesh creeping all the way up your arms and tears filling your eyes just because something was so unbelievably beautiful? And after that, what happened? Could you admit the feeling to yourself and – heaven forbid – to others as well? Without cracking jokes about getting old and sentimental? Good. Because honest appreciation of all things beautiful is the way forward…"

I would love to include the entire mission statement here, but brevity is at times also the way forward and anyway: you can read it on www.beautywithoutirony.com. As I sent the manifesto out to artists (still not quite knowing what to expect) I included the following key words, the things I wanted Beauty Without Irony to be all about:

"Love, patience, respect, inspiration, quirkiness, hope, individuality, humanity, crossing borders, passion, tenderness, reflection, spirituality, evolution, friendship, creativity, joy, courage, revelation, uniqueness, understanding, pride, knowledge, intuition, fun, links, surprises, humility, ideas, optimism, synergy, kindness, co-operation, cross-thinking, the pleasure of creating."

Having said all that – and much more – I sent out the text to all my friends who then forwarded it to their acquaintances and so on. In the accompanying letter I asked for feedback and examples of things that they considered to be beauty without irony. Well, it's a good thing I have a large mailbox (both virtual and metal) because before long the replies came flooding in: statements, pictures, artwork, music and fashion of course. One of the first was writer / philosopher Alain de Botton, who said that my statement summarised exactly what his work was all about. I seemed to have struck a chord. Since I didn't expect all those replies and as the project didn't have an actual goal, I decided to put as much of the material as possible on a website – which in turn encouraged even more people to send in their own idea of beauty without irony. In 2005 we even staged an actual exhibition during the Super! Triennial in Hasselt (in shops, bars and even launderettes, all places that should definitely feature art as far as I'm concerned), but I'm rushing ahead of myself. Again.

I saw it all happen during that glorious spring of 2001 and I was amazed and extremely pleased, but ever so slightly frustrated as well. Inspiring people to create really beautiful things is fantastic, but what to do with the results? So we put it on a site. Nice. We staged exhibitions. Wonderful. But where could we go from there? Apart from (re)introducing beauty in its purest form to people, BWI didn't have any positive effects at all. What if I could somehow take the idea one step further and harness all this creativity so that it would actually make a difference in the world?

CHAPTER THREE

Often, all it takes to make the shift from 'if' to 'how' is a chance encounter and that's exactly what happened in 2001 when jeans brand Evisu asked me to help them organize a fundraiser. The idea was to ask Belgian designers and celebrities to customize a pair of Evisu jeans or a denim jacket which would then be auctioned off. For the company, it was mainly a PR exercise but for me, it was a golden opportunity to put a social angle on all this new-found creativity. I even got to pick my own charity and with Peter Verhelst in mind I chose the HIV/AIDS research department of the Antwerp-based Institute of Tropical Medicine. The ITM has been on the forefront of this research for many years – and had made several important breakthroughs – but unfortunately those achievements still didn't generate sufficient funding. So it was an easy choice. Happily, the project – which I dubbed Designers Do Denim – went very well indeed. An impressive array of designers, artists and even politicians participated (if you're into name-dropping you'll find an exhaustive list of people who have contributed to BWI / DDD / DAA in this book) and a lot of money was raised during the auction, which took place as 2001 drew to a close. All of the revenue soon found its way to the ITM and everybody was happy with the results of Designers Do Denim, not in the least myself.

In short, while Beauty Without Irony had given me a sense of purpose, Designers Do Denim proved that creative energy (and, therefore, beauty) could be used in order to make a better world, notably raising money for a good cause: the research into and prevention of HIV/AIDS.

For the consistency of this story, it would have been nice if things now shifted into a higher gear, but that was not to be. While the contributions to BWI kept flooding in over the years, I still had to make a living – I wanted to leave the entire fashion writing thing behind me, but at the time I thought that was taking one step too far. I was also put off by the idea that I would earn my keep – however modest – from charity work, yet it was obvious that I would have to spend all my time doing just that: work on charity projects, if I wanted to achieve anything worthwhile.

However, in 2004 I was asked to organize yet another fundraiser. This time legendary dance temple Café d'Anvers was celebrating its 15th birthday and they wanted to do their bit for charity. I would ask a host of designers and musicians – this time the list included international stars such as DJ Dimitri From Paris and Calvin Klein – to create their own design to print on T-shirts. Again, all the proceeds would go to the ITM. I decided to call this project Designers against AIDS. It all went very smoothly and when the event was over, I found that we still had a few boxes of tees left. Not being one to let anything go to waste (must have something to do with my Dutch roots) I took them to the Premium Fashion Fair in Berlin. As I was talking to the visitors, I came to the conclusion that most of them didn't have a clue what HIV and safe sex were all about. Since the great prevention campaigns of the late '80s had gradually faded away, ignorance had settled in people's minds once again. Clearly, something had to be done and it was at that point, on a dreary February afternoon in 2005, that I decided to put all my eggs in one basket. I was going to turn DAA into a fully-fledged brand and from now on, I would dedicate all my energy to the project. This included establishing a clothing line, setting up an office, building a network and liaising with similar organisations. I felt as if I didn't have a choice in the matter.

CHAPTER FOUR

It all sounds both so simple and so very pretentious now. But it didn't back then. It just seemed like the only way forward to me. My feelings were vindicated by the swiftness of subsequent events. I enlisted the help of Javier Barcala, who came from MTV in Spain and who had all the contacts to the music world I could only dream of, as my creative director. In August 2006 our first collection, sponsored by Umbro and featuring art work by the likes of Robert Smith of The Cure and Faithless, hit the shops. From then on until spring-summer 2009 we brought out two collections a year, the later ones even included underwear, bed linen and swimwear.

The creative results were excellent but I soon realised the financial ones weren't quite as impressive. Being on a mission and having a clear sense of purpose doesn't necessarily make you a good salesperson, that much was obvious. I found it very hard to focus on everything at the same time: the creative aspect, finding new designers and celebrities, the production, distribution, communication... It all had to be done without a budget or sufficient staff and that meant that some aspects didn't quite get the attention they deserved. And to be honest, I'm much better at writing motivational emails to superstars than at discussing the finer points of garment distribution in Japan.

As early as the autumn of 2006 I realised that DAA needed a solid partner for a parallel project, but on a much grander scale. Something that would really make an impact on people's minds as well as on the coffers of non-profit HIV/AIDS organisations that are similar to ours, both in Belgium and in other countries. At the time, I was planning a second line of clothes – again

based on the designs of pop culture heroes, which I had already tentatively called Fashion against AIDS (FAA). For this, I absolutely wanted to work with a major player in the clothing industry, one that could take the entire production aspect off our hands. That way, we could focus on the creative side, the communication and the actual setting up of campaigns. In other words: 'they' would produce, market and sell the clothes while DAA would provide the artists / celebrities, the designs and the ideology. But we weren't just looking for a large, international company with massive marketing and retailing resources; it also had to be flexible enough to grab an opportunity when it was put to them.
It didn't take me long to figure out that Swedish retail giant Hennes & Mauritz (H&M) fitted the bill very nicely indeed.

But how does one approach one of the largest clothing companies in the world, especially one that was known to have supported good causes in the past, and which would probably be inundated with hundreds of business proposals? I couldn't just barge into their headquarters with the DAA portfolio saying: "This is a project I believe we can both benefit from. It's got all it needs as far as key selling points are concerned: a good cause with a bit of an edge, great designs and contributions by lots and lots of pop icons." That wouldn't do at all. I didn't have their address, for one thing. That's how I ended up calling the H&M customer service. The girl on the other end of the line kindly gave me the contact info of the 'Bizarre Proposals and Suggestions Department' (I'm not sure that's exactly what they called it) and I was about to thank her and hang up when, as an afterthought, I asked if she could put me through to the Creative Director. Much to my surprise the girl – presumably thinking that someone that mad must be important – immediately transferred me to his office. He made an appointment without further ado and within weeks I found myself sitting at a very expensive Swedish table together with Javier, being eyed up with curiosity by an impressive array of 'directors', 'vice-presidents' and the like. "Well," I said. "This is a project I believe we can both benefit from..."
We were on a roll again.
The question I'm asked most often is why I started with Designers against AIDS in the first place.
You might think I find it easy to answer that one by now. Unfortunately, I don't. The thing is: it was an emotional decision, not a rational one. It wasn't even a decision, it was more like an emotional process that somehow turned into a project. And as you will know, it's already hard enough to explain what you feel when you are feeling it, never mind years after the event.

CHAPTER FIVE

Or, in this case, a series of events. What was I feeling during that infamous fashion show in Paris? What was I feeling when Peter passed away? What was I feeling during the graduation show of Serkan Sarier at the Antwerp Fashion Academy? What was I feeling when I started to realize that there was so much ignorance and arrogance in the fashion business? What was I feeling when the creative and selfless contributions to my very first fundraiser started pouring in, and most of them actually came from that very same fashion world? Or when I found myself addressing a UNFPA, UNESCO or UNICEF meeting in New York or Paris? And what was I feeling when I did my first research into the subject, and only got blank stares when I asked my children what they knew about HIV/AIDS? It's very hard to put all these things into a nicely gift-wrapped answer. Let's just say that it all had a profound impact on me and that, as time went by and things started happening, I felt that what I was doing was right. It's as simple as that, when I come to think of it. It felt right. It simply was the only way forward for me.

Another question that pops up quite frequently during interviews is "why do you use fashion as the means to enhance AIDS awareness among young people?" Part of the explanation lies in the question itself. Along with celebrities, music, the internet, art and social media, fashion is a hugely important part of popular culture. In fact DAA uses all of the above in order to get our message across, because those are the things teenagers are interested in. It means more to them if for instance Timbaland says that safe sex is cool than when their mother tells them the exact same thing. Which is a pity because the overall knowledge about HIV/AIDS – and STDs in general – among young people is still nothing like it should be. A lot of work remains to be done there. But at least it's a start and, fortunately, big companies as well as the media are now starting to realize the importance of raising AIDS awareness again, because the effects of the first wave of campaigns in the late '80s and early '90s have completely died down. Young people who were babies then – and therefore missed out on those campaigns – are now reaching the age where they become sexually active. As the number of infections continues to rise, it's becoming personal for more and more people. But only a few years ago, people and companies had a totally different attitude towards HIV prevention campaigns. I still remember the reply of the marketing director of a large fashion corporation when I asked for their support: "We can't possibly support an AIDS-awareness campaign; that would be bad for our brand image. Can't you do something for children with cancer instead?" The one good thing about getting letters like that is that they only encourage me to double my efforts. Ignorance certainly is not bliss in a case like this.

CHAPTER SIX

For a while, DAA mainly occupied itself with the fashion collections and liaising with other organisations involved – or rather: specialized – in HIV/AIDS prevention programmes. However, I felt that DAA also had an educational role to play – if only to ensure that our work will become sustainable. That's why I decided to set up the first 'International HIV/AIDS Awareness Education Centre'. The IHAEC is housed in a building in Antwerp that we specifically purchased for that goal, using the donations of H&M. The idea is that young people from all over the world can come to us for a two-month course and take part in creative and practical workshops. We will also set up one specific project with them, like organizing a fashion show with national designers in their own country, or a music festival. This way, the students – who will be selected in cooperation with local HIV/AIDS organizations worldwide – will be able to learn all there is to know about setting up projects of their own when they return home: production, communication, logistics, finances and so on. Yes, the programme even includes the things that we were apprehensive about during the early days of DAA and made us enter a partnership with H&M; it turns out that we are quick learners as far as practicalities are concerned. Apart from benefitting from our own experience, the students will also have the opportunity to take part in classes that are hosted by various experts who will equally provide them loads of useful information and techniques.

At the end of their course, the students-turned-DAA ambassadors will return home, where they will be able to set up their own projects, as well as pass on the skills they have learned. And they'll be able to do it in a way that appeals to their peers, as they combine their newly-acquired expertise with their own in-depth knowledge of local customs, sensitivities and tastes. Being active members of a local HIV/AIDS organization, they'll also have all the support they need and they can of course always get in touch with DAA if and when they need additional information or contacts. Not everybody is strong (or crazy) enough to take on HIV prevention campaigns on their own!

The fact that we are inviting students from all over the world is very important as well because DAA still focuses mainly on Western Europe and the United States at the moment. But of course HIV/AIDS is a global problem and it must be tackled accordingly, so we have to take cultural differences into account. European pop culture – our own field of expertise – does not have much in common with Indian, Chinese or South-American pop culture, Lady Gaga and Coldplay notwithstanding. So we really need people from those countries to work on their own projects and spread the word in a language their compatriots understand. That way, we hope that DAA will become a worldwide phenomenon in a couple of years.

Needless to say, the IHAEC is our top priority at the moment and we're all working non-stop in order to make it operational as soon as possible. The end – or rather, the brand new start – is finally in sight and that's nothing short of a miracle.
As is the case with all projects where real estate is involved, unexpected problems have arisen continuously and the actual cost of the renovations is giving the original budget a delicately manicured middle finger. I spent quite a few sleepless night worrying. That's why setting up a second center would be utter madness – we are planning the opening in Los Angeles in 2013.

In the meantime, we will of course continue to collaborate with H&M on our global Fashion against AIDS collections, as well as introduce a new range of beautifully packaged DAA condoms that we hope to sell worldwide, as this is the next logical step in HIV prevention. If everybody used them, the number of HIV infections would go down dramatically. It's as simple as that. So turning the purchase and use of condoms into a cool thing to do in young people's minds is obviously a priority.

DAA is also partnering with the Global Business Coalition on HIV/AIDS, Tuberculosis and Malaria – an organisation that was set up by the likes of Ted Turner and Bill Gates, including multinational companies such as Coca-Cola, Pfizer and Nike. Through the GBC, we hope to branch out into other fields of pop culture. After all, you simply can't do enough or use too many channels to raise HIV/AIDS awareness. We'll also continue to strengthen our links with other non-profit organisations so that we can not only coordinate our efforts but also create campaigns together and share our experiences. Because if there's something I have learned over the years with DAA, it must be the importance of networking, synergies and solidarity. We are extremely proud of the fact that part of the FAA donations are now going to UNFPA, MTV's Staying Alive Foundation and Youthaids, to help with their global HIV prevention work. We're talking hundreds of thousands of dollars per year here, money that those organisations desperately need but wouldn't have gotten otherwise.

WRAP IT UP

I sometimes get asked: "When does it end?" and my standard answer is "On the day that there are no more new HIV infections." That may sound a bit flippant or naive, but it's true: DAA still has so much work to do and so many people to reach... I realize that I may not be there to see the glorious day that HIV is a thing of the past, but I also know that other people will continue to spread the message in a variety of ways. And their number continues to grow – either directly through the IHAEC, or indirectly because a DAA campaign made them think for a bit. Once you start doing that, it's only a small step to taking real action. I know. I've been there. Again, it's the only way forward.

CALL TO ARMS

By buying this book you've already made an important contribution to the future of Designers against AIDS and we would like to thank you for that. But in case you 'borrowed' it from someone else's coffee table or if you would like to make another contribution – financial, creative or otherwise – then of course your efforts will be very much appreciated. Please visit http://www.designersagainstaids.com and find out what you can do.

FASHION AGAINST AIDS

In October 2007, when I still was head of design at H&M, we announced a press release about the first edition of Fashion against AIDS, our collaboration with the Belgian NGO Designers against AIDS (DAA), founded **"MARGARETA VAN DEN BOSCH"** by Ninette Murk who came to present the idea to our company in Stockholm a year before that. Stars such as Rihanna, Timbaland, Rufus Wainwright and Katharine Hamnett created colourful prints with safe sex messages for T-shirts and the collection and campaign were very succesful worldwide.

Meanwhile, Fashion against AIDS is entering its 4th year and I believe that it has made young people think again about AIDS, in a fashionable way. I'm sure that I'm not alone in saying that everybody working at H&M is extremely proud to be involved in such a great project.

In June 2010 I met Ninette personally at a brunch for the fashion students of the Antwerp Academy, where I realized that creativity is very important to both of us – and also to discover and support young talents.

With the donation money of Fashion against AIDS, DAA has renovated a building in Antwerp that will act as an education center to train young students from all over the world in how to make pop culture based HIV prevention campaigns aimed at their peers, so their work becomes sustainable. Of course we hope that AIDS will soon be a thing of the past, but until then, creating safe sex campaigns that appeal to youth so that they protect themselves and their partners is the only way forward. And I'm proud of the fact that H&M has been – and still is – instrumental in helping to make this happen!

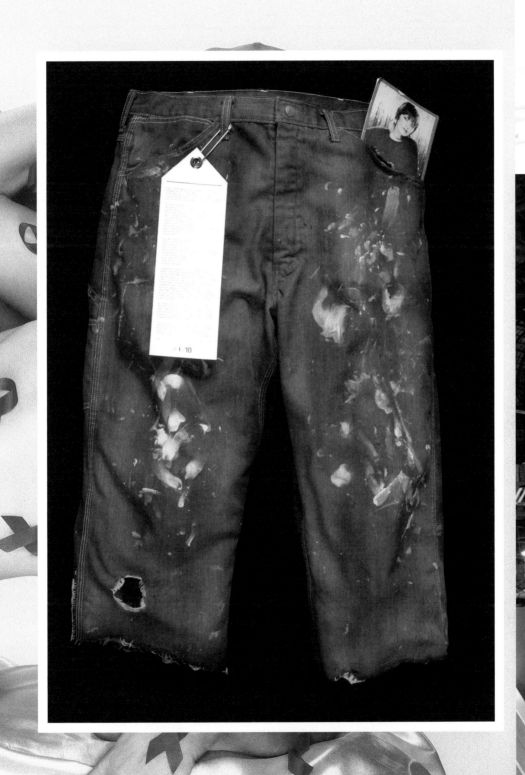

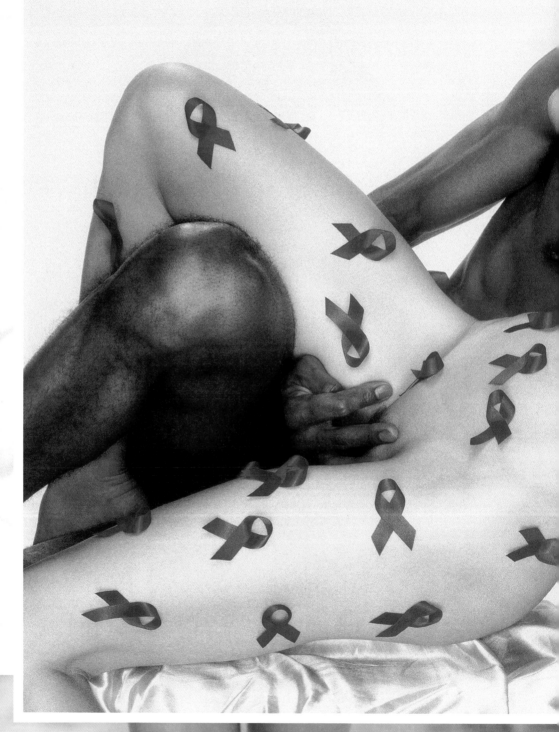

AIDS IS A
WEAPON
OF MASS
DESTRUCTION

USE A CONDOM
FAITHLESS

STOP
AND
THINK

ボディ ¥2,490
DESIGN: KATY PERRY

FASHION AGAINST AIDS

T-shirt
14,90
DESIGN: B?

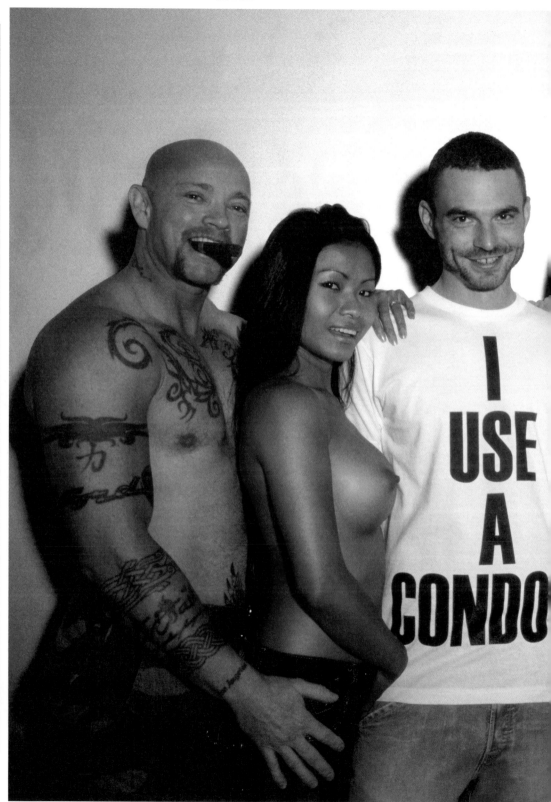

BY THE TIME THIS TRAM REACHES THE NEXT STOP
THERE WILL BE 5 NEW CASES OF HIV WORLDWIDE.
PROTECT!
YOURSELF DAA

www.designersagainstaids.com

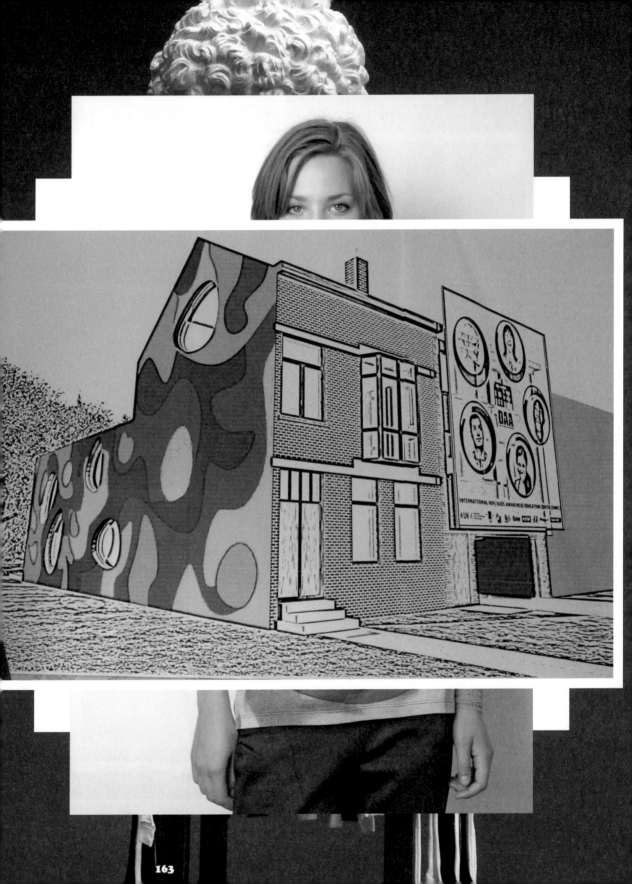

www.designersagainstaids.com

chicks on speed

DAA
www.designersagainstaids.com

campaigns in their countries of origin. More info: **www.inaec.org**

170

campaigns in their countries of origin. More info. www.inaec.org

172

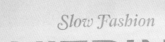

Slow Fashion

VITRINE

Slow Fashion
VITRINE

EEN VERANTWOORD
MODEPARCOURS IN ANTWERPEN

05 – 26
JUNI 2010

MEER INFO OP
WWW.FFI.BE/VITRINE

PERSONALIZED EDITION
created by
Zoltàn Gerliczki
for

FOLDER BESCHIKBAAR BIJ
ANTWERPEN TOERISME EN CONGRES
GROTE MARKT 13 – 2000 ANTWERPEN
CENTRAAL STATION – 2018 ANTWERPEN

Dear BP,
If you don't have the right tools in your toolbox, you don't drill.

Using pop culture to make the world a better place.

DAA
www.designersagainstaids.com

Thank you for supporting our
International HIV/AIDS Awareness Education Center.
More info: www.ihaec.org

This campaign was created by Addictlab.com to support the opening of the International HIV/AIDS Awareness Education Center (IHAEC). The training center in Antwerp, Belgium will host students from all over the world and teach them how to set up successful HIV prevention and awareness programs, using the same pop culture based methods used by DesignersAgainstAids. The students will be taking this knowledge home, to build up equally successful campaigns in their countries of origin. More info: **www.ihaec.org**

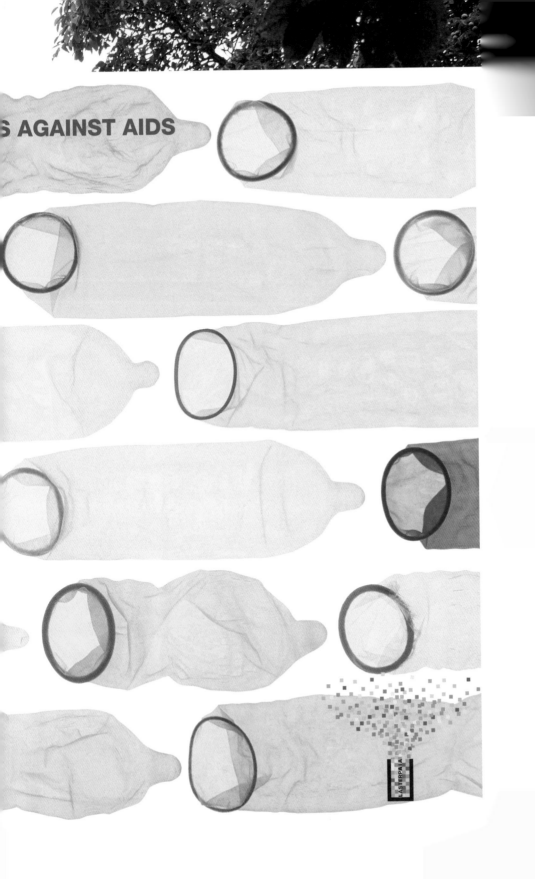

S AGAINST AIDS

CREDITS

BEAUTY WITHOUT IRONY CREDITS

p12
Daniel Riera
'Zachary'
Fashion editor James Valeri
Hair Marco Santini
Make-Up Yasuo Yoshikawa.
Model Zachary (VNYModels)
www.danielriera.com

p13
Erwin Olaf
'Hotel Moscow - Room 168'
www.erwinolaf.com

p14
Teun Voeten
'Afghan Doves'
Local Afghans feeding
the ever present white pigeons
at the Blue Mosque.
Mazar-e-Sharif, Afghanistan,
November 1996
www.teunvoeten.com

p15
Jimmy Kets
'Elvis'
From the series 'Shot in Flanders'
www.jimmykets.be

p16
Yoko Ono
'Imagine Peace'
2010
www.imaginepeace.com

p17
Pat Kurs
'Combface'
www.patkurs.com

p18
Zoltan Gerliczki
'Dervish'
2010
www.zoltanportfolio.com

p19
Ronald Van der Hilst
'Falling Drop'
Photo Michael James O'Brien
2010
www.ronaldvanderhilst.com
www.michaeljamesobrien.com

p20
Douglas Friedman
'Jellyfish in a Tank'
2010
www.douglasfriedman.net

p21
Eva Gödel
'Piet'
www.chewingthesun.com

p22
Nick Hannes
'Untitled'
www.nickhannes.be

p23
Sarah Van Marcke
'Japan'
Fumihiko Maki
www.outlandish-photo.be

p24
Diane Pernet
'Nobuyoshi Araki'
www.ashadedviewonfashion.com

p25
Jef Paepen
From the series 'Introspection'
www.jefpaepen.be

p26
Layla Aerts
'Firanka'
www.laylaaerts.be

p27
Karim Rashid
'Self Portrait'
www.karimrashid.com

p28
Meta by Tord Boontje
Design by Studio Tord Boontje
for Meta,
Photo Meta
www.tordboontje.com

p29
Elke Boon
'Marie'
2007
www.elkeboon.be

p30
Sandrine Dulermo &
Michael Labica
'Dita'
Courtesy of Sam Kloss/
Absynth Photo
www.absynthphoto.com

p31
Moby
'Untitled'
2008
www.moby.com

p32
Martin Bing
'Untitled'
Model Wouter Bleyen
Designer Ken Crombez

p33
Vincent W. Gagliostro
'Breathing'
www.gagliostro.com

p34
Dominik Gigler
'Night at Brasilia Airport'
www.gigler.com

p35
Mick Traen
'Carpe Diem'
'Carpe Diem' or, living in the now.
"That's what I like about all dogs
and learn from mine every day."
www.micktraen.com

p36
Lars Stephan
'Berlin #1'
www.larsstephan.com

p37
Frank Horvat
'Malte & Mona'
2008
www.horvatland.com

p38
Gianluca Tamorri
'Portrait in a Flowered Shirt'
www.gianlucatamorri.com

p39
Sara Claes
'Untitled'
From the series 'Une histoire
personnelle'
2008
www.saraclaes.be

p40
Arpaïs du Bois
'Petit Morceau de Ciel en
Forme de Désir'
2010
www.arpais.com

p41
Romulo Fialdinini
'Oscar Niemeyer's hands'
Art Director Danniel Rangel
www. romulofialdini.com

p42
Dirk Swartenbroekx
'True Colours'
Namibia, 2009

p43
Valérie Servant
'BIRIBI part 1/2/3'
On the last photo, with the most
tattoos, you will see that the boy
has the letter S for South on the
neck, underneath he has a N for
North,and on the shoulders the E
for East, and O for Ouest (west).
When you look closely, you will
see that E and O are reversed,
meaning that East is on the right
side instead of the left side...This
is done on purpose, it's not that I
don't know where East and Ouest
should be, but at the opposite
I wanted to include a tip in the
picture: the fact is that at the time
in Biribi, the prisoners used to
tattoo each other in very difficult
situations: stress (and pain). It was
forbidden so they had to hide and
be fast. Also, some of them would
sometimes tattoo themselves with

mirror (or whatever they would and that had a reflection) and with a mirror you see things reversed, the reason why this kind of mistake would happen to them. I selected these images because at Biribi a lot of gay men were imprisoned, just because of their sexual orientation.

p44
Hannelore Knuts
'Eye Flash'

p45
Franky Claeys
'After the fight'
www.frankyclaeys.com

p46
Virgili Jubero for Noe
Duchafour Lawrance
'Objets empruntés'
Concept, design and art direction
Noé Duchaufour-Lawrance
Photo Virgili Jubero
www.virgilijubero.com

p47
Iké Udé
'Flower Portraits, Calla Lily'
2010
www.arudemagazine.com

p48
Tim Van Steenbergen
'Erda in 'Das Rheingold' for
La Scala'
www.timvansteenbergen.com

p49
Jason (Woei-Ping) Chen
'Untitled'
from the series 'One of us'
www.jasonbc.com

p50
Wouter Van Vaerenbergh
'Untitled'
www.woutervanvaerenbergh.com

p51
Filip Van Roe
'Zoë'
www.initials-la.com

p52
Riitta Päiväläinen
'Windsnest'
www.helsinkischool.fi

p53
Elisabeth Novick
'Untitled'
www.elisabethnovick.com

p54
Diego Franssens
'Mona'
www.diego.be

p55
Xander Ferreira
'Hunt of the Gazelle'
self portrait from the series 'The
Status of Greatness' -
"To write an interesting story
within history, is a true love for an
adventurous life."
www.yogazelle.com

p56
Dominic Sio
'Wrinkles'
www.stimulionline.com

p57
Franky Verdickt
from the series 'Atopia'
www.frankyverdickt.be

p58
Chris Plytas
'Mathieu'
Ségur, 2009
www.chrisplytas.com

p59
Ben Van Alboom
'Lana'

p60
Mark Titchner
'In The Days'
www.marktitchnerstudio.com

p61
Filip Naudts
'De onschuld'
From the series 'La clé du boudoir'
www.filipnaudts.be
www.guardalafotografia.be

p62
Piet Raemdonck
'Bloemenvazen'
2009
www.pietraemdonck.com

p63
Thomas Vanhaute
'Fisherman on Lake Inle,
Myanmar'
www.thomasvanhaute.com

p64
Luiz Carlos Barreto
'Marilyn Monroe'
Fox Studios, Hollywood,
USA, 1959
Thanks to Lucy Barreto, Tássia
Milly, Tereza Athayde, LC Barreto
www.lcbarreto.com

p65
Tom and Bill Kaulitz
'Paris, taken from Tokio Hotel
stage'
www.tokiohotel.com

p66
Vlieger & Vandam
'Tote Skull'
www.vliegervandam.com

p67
Jamie Brennan
'Yulia'
www.jamiebrennan.com

p68
Felix Richter
'Caracara Falcon, Pantanal'
Brazil, 2009
www.felixrichter.com

p69
Tom Tosseyn
'It's Like When I Dream'
www.tomtosseyn.com

p70
Jarno Kettunen
'Boudicca'
Boudicca Couture
2008
www.jarnok.com

p71
Ali Mahdavi
'My Baby'
Art direction Stefano Canulli
www.alimahdavi.net

p72
Antonio Paladino
for Serkan Sarier
'Ballet Room'
Art direction Serkan Sarier
www.antomiopaladino.com

p73
Jean Claude Wouters
'Marc Jacobs Portrait'
www.jeanclaudewouters.eu

p74
Peggy Sirota
'Twins'
www.peggysirota.com

p75
Andy Wauman
'Adios Paradise'
Courtesy Deweer Gallery, Belgium.
www.andywauman.be

p76
Annelies De Mey
'Untitled'
www.anneliesdemey.com

p77
Thierry Van Biesen
'HeadBack'
Stylist Marianne Ghantous
Makeup Linda Ohrstrom
Hair Juan-Carlos Perianez
September 2002
www.thierryvanbiesen.com

p78
Sophie Rata
'Exingeois'
Dress Maison Anna Heylen
www.sophierata.be
www.annaheylen.be

p79
Photographer Unknown
'Vera Valdez,
Coco Chanel's muse'
Maison Chanel
1962

p80
Daniel Jackson
'Jeniel'
2010
www.daniel-jackson.co.uk

p81
Marc Atlan
'Blood Simple'
www.marcatlan.com

p82
Monika Macken
'Love in a strange country'
www.monikamacken.be

p83
Ole Stragier
'Honorate'
www.ole-stragier.com

p84
Wendy Marijnissen
'Devilles Harem Girls'
Designer Murielle Scherre
wmarijnissen.photoshelter.com

p85
Glenn Glasser
'Kiss No Bruise'
www.glennglasser.com

p86
Candice Mai Khanh Nguyen
'Beetle'
Sapa, Vietnam, May 2009

p87
Tinko Czetwertynski
'Two moons in one night'
2010
www.beirutlove.com
www.czetwertynski.net

p88
Demna Gvasalia
for Peter Hornstein
'Elisabeth & Rudolf'
www.peterhornstein.com

p89
Francesco Carrozzini
for Jordan Betten/Lost Art
'Untitled'
2010
www.bettenart.com

p90
Jürgen Nefzger
'Nocturne'
Courtesy Galerie Françoise Paviot,
Paris, 2008
www.juergennefzger.com

p96
Michel Vaerewijck 'Voyou'
Part of 'slow-photographer'
Michel Vaerewijck's collection of
nudes, each one safely stored in a
minimalist wooden box. The glass
plate is a unique direct positive
without duplicate and a silent
witness to a visual introspection of
the photographer & the model.
www.maxepyan.com

p92
Eva Vermandel
'Cli, after swimming'
June 2010
www.evavermandel.com

p93
Joss McKinley
'Stretch-Maryville'
Newport, 2009
www.jossmckinley.com

p94
Annick Geenen
'Heaven'
Jewelry Heaven Tanudiredja -
Model Amélie Lens
www.annickgeenen.be
www.heaventanudiredja.be

p95
Karin Hanssen
'The Approach'
www.karin-hanssen.be

p96
Ellie Van Den Brande
'Droom'
www.ellievdb.com

p97
Tom and Bill Kaulitz
Tokio Hotel
'In the plane to Male'
'Clouds'
www.tokiohotel.com

p98
Morgan Showalter
'Back'
From the multi-media project
'Tattoo', Model and Tattoo
Designer Heather Joi Baker
2009
www.morganshowalter.com

p99
Wayne Hemingway
'Dog Sledding Trip'
www.vintageatgoodwood.com

p100
Jessica Antola
'Mom'
www.antolaphoto.com

p101
Bert Danckaert
'Simple Present #211'
Cape Town, 2008
www.bert-danckaert.be

p102
Emmanuel Laurent
**'Enfant faisant des Ronds
dans l'Eau'**
www.emmanuel-laurent.com

p103
Titus Simoens
'Grand Canyon, Arizona, USA'
www.titussimoens.be

p104
Werner Van Reck
'Plage Granville, Bretagne'
Digital retouching Luc Janssens,
Pixco Antwerpen
2009
www.wernervanreck.com

p105
Deborah Irmas
'Vietnamese girls'

p106
Danny Veys
'Untitled'
www.photolimits.be

p107
Kimiko Yoshida
'Delacroix'
www.kimiko.fr

p108
Javier Barcala
'The Fields'
2010
www.lafortunastudio.com

p109
Nadine Tasseel
'Untitled'
www.galeriebaudelaire.be

p110
Frances Joossens
'Untitled'
francesjoossens.blogspot.com

p111
Piet Goethals
'Untitled'

p112
Olaf Breuning
'Clouds'
www.olafbreuning.com

p113
Valéry Grancher
'Spitsbergen'
www.valerygrancher.vg

p114
Jamie Campbell
'Untitled'
jamiecampbellphotography.com

p115
Andres Hubertus Ilse
'Veruschka'
Veruschka Self-Portraits
Performed by Vera Lehndorf
www.veruschkaselfportraits.com

DESIGNERS AGAINST AIDS CREDITS

p134
**Designers Do Denim
by Raf Simons**
Photo Jean Francois Carly
2001

p135
**Martin Margiela
for Designers Do Denim**
Photo Michel Comte
Model Alek Wek
2001

p136
**Piotr Piskozub
Knitting against Aids**
Photo O'Brien & Gerliczki
2009

p137
**Ninette Murk
Knitting against Aids**
Photo O'Brien & Gerliczki
2009

p138 – 139
Lee Cooper 100 Auction
Art by Dino Dinco
For the 100 year Lee Cooper
project we asked young designers
and artists to customize denim
pieces, with benefits of the
auction going to the Red Cross
in France and Designers against
AIDS. Artist, filmmaker and AIDS
activist Dino Dinco from Los
Angeles asked 10 seropositive
artists to each customize their
favorite pair of jeans and the
results can be seen here –
a great and thoughtful concept!
2008

p140 – 141
Erwin Olaf for DAA
2007

p142
**Kim Peers in Faithless
for DAA design**
2005

p143
Faithless canvas
Antwerp's Central Station
200 m2 large
2005

p144
**T-shirt by Paul Snowden
for DAA/Sense Organics**
Photo Marc Lagrange
Model Anouck Lepère
2008

p145
**T-shirt by Nice Collective for
DAA/Sense Organics**
Photo Michael James O'Brien
Model Olivier Chapusette
2009

p146
FAA 1 Ziggy Marley
Photo Daniel Jackson
2008

p147
FAA 1 Katharine Hamnett
Photo John Scarisbrick
2008

p148
FAA 2 Dita Von Teese
Photo Daniel Jackson

p149
FAA 3
Photo Dan Martensen
2010

p150 – 151
FAA 2 Tokio Hotel
Photo Daniel Jackson
2009

p152
FAA 2
Billboard in Tokyo
Japan, 2009

p153
FAA 2
The H&M marketing team at work
in a bus shelter in Amsterdam,
sticking condoms on a campaign
poster, for people to take away.
2009

p154
**Mistral for DAA bedlinen
designed by Vive la Fête**
2009

p155
Design by Playboy for DAA
Bread & Butter Charity Store
2007

p156
Mano Mundo
Photo Zoltan Gerliczki
2010

p157
Mano Mundo
Ninette Murk and
her husband Peter Gubbels
2010

p158 – 159
Porn stars for DAA
Photo Nils Rodekamp
2007

p160
Antwerp Pride
June 2010

p161
Taking the DAA tram
Concept Michael James O'Brien
Design Tom Tosseyn
Photo Zoltan Gerliczki
June 2010

p162
IHAEC construction site
Dallila Hermans
Photo Candice Mai Khanh Nguyen

p163
IHAEC
Design B-bis/B-architecten

p164
IHAEC construction
Photo Dominic Sio
June 2010

p165
Christophe Coppens for DAA
Photo Studio Verne
2008

p166
**Condom and T-shirt designed
by Chicks on Speed for DAA**
From a series with 10 artists/
musicians made for MJA (now
called Joetz)
2007

p167
**Hannelore Knuts in a DAA
festival T-shirt with bags and
purses from the DAA Thai bag
project**
Photo Michael James O'Brien
2009

p168
Cheek Magazine cover
Photo Hamish Kippen
May 2008

p169
Six Scents perfumes
Nr2 by Bernhard Willhelm

p170
**DAA ringbinders for
Timmermans Office supplies**
This one is designed by Robert
Smith, singer/guitar player with
The Cure
2006 – 2007

p171
**DAA customized T-shirt
by Zoltan Gerliczki**
2009

p172
**F*cking Dinosaurs design
by Bernhard Willhelm**
Photo Nils Rodekamp
2007

p173
**The late Percy Irausquin in his
design for DAA/A Fair**
2006

p174
Vitrine 'Slow Fashion'
Ronald van der Hilst for DAA
Antwerp, 2010

p175
Vitrine 'Slow Fashion'
Poster by Zoltan Gerliczki
Antwerp, 2010

p176
**Online DAA condom
advertisement from a series**
By Jan Van Mol @ Addictlab.com

p177
DAA ads by Nick Lovell
For Talenthouse
2010
www.nicklovell.com

p178 – 179
Oliviero Toscani
For DAA
2007

p180 – 181
IHAEC
Design B-bis/B-architecten
Photo Michaël James O'Brien
September 2010

OTHER

OVERVIEW PROJECTS DESIGNERS AGAINST AIDS 2001 › 2011

Autumn 2001
Designers Do Denim
(see p134 – 135)

November 2004
15 years Café D'Anvers

May 2005
First DAA collection
(see p142)

June 2005
Madrid Gay Pride

Barcelona, July 2005
CMYK Magazine fair

Los Angeles, September 2005
Launch party DAA

Antwerp, September 2005
**Los Niños
DAA awareness party**

**Exhibition at Amsterdam
Fashion Week**

Hasselt, September 2005
Super! art exhibition

Antwerp, December 1st 2005
**Faithless canvas
at Central Station**

June 2006
DAA collection S/S 2007
(see p134, 172)

August 2006
Timmermans ring binders
(see p170)

Antwerp, September 2006
Vitrine

Friends of DAA

October 2006
DAA customized collection
(see p171)

Antwerp, November 2006
**Fashion Model contest
at Central Station**

Berlin, November 2006
Ben Q Siemens auction

December 2006
300% Design book

Lille, 2007
Maison Mode

2007
Dawanda online store

May 2007
Erwin Olaf campaign photo
(see p140 – 141)

Antwerp, June 2007
European Gay Games
(see p166)

July 2007
Belgian Pop Line condoms

Antwerp, July 2007
Café Capital exhibition

Antwerp, July 2007
**S/S 2006 collection in
collaboration with A Fair**
(see p173)

Berlin, July 2007
**S/S 2007 collection
worn by porn stars**
(see p158 – 159)

Barcelona, July 2007
**Bread & Butter
charity store collection**
(see p155)

August 2007
**Timmermans ring binders
2nd edition**
(see p170)

Antwerp, September 2007
Vitrine

Brussels, October 2007
**DAA@ Modo Parcours Brussels
Monsieur K**

Brussels, October 2007
**DAA@ Modo Parcours Brussels
FAIR Store**

December 1st 2007
AIDS info Market Brussels

January 31st 2008
**First edition
Fashion Against AIDS**
(see p146 – 147)

January 2008
DAA F/W 2008 collection
(see p145)

January 2008
Models against AIDS

Hamburg, May 2008
Trendbüro conference

May 2008
Cheek Magazine image
(see p168)

May 2008
**Promotional video
by Mick Traen**

Brussels, May 2008
**Cointreau fundraising event
with Dita Von Teese**

September 2008
**Bozar Brussels expo 'It's Not
Only Rock 'N Roll, Baby'**

May until August 2008
**International Benicassim/
Spain Festival**

September 2008
Expose NYC sales booth

September 2008
**Clowns Without Borders
Sweden (cruise)**

Paris, September 2008
**Lee Cooper global denim
charity project & auction**
(see p138 – 139)

September 2008
Photo shoot Anouck Lepère
(see p144)

October 2008
Six Scents perfume
(see p169)

Antwerp, December 1st 2008
IHAEC soft opening

February 2009
New website DAA

May 2009
DAA Festival T-shirts
(see p167)

April 2009
**DAA awareness video clip
André J**

Circle of friends

May 2009
**NYC against HIV Health
Symposium**

Belgium, May 2009
Mano Mundo festival

Antwerp, May 2009
Zappa music event

Belgium, May 2009
Baggit

May 28th 2009
**Second edition Fashion
Against AIDS**
(see p148, 150 – 153)

Spain, August 20th 2009
DAA safe sex party in Tenerife

eptember 2009
Mistral bed linen
(see p154)

Thailand, September 2009
Thai bags & skirts
Life Home Project Phuket
(see p167)

Tunisia, September 2009
Y-Peer convention

Antwerp, November 10th 2009
Vila Cabral

Antwerp, November –
January 2009
Safe sex poster campaign

September – December 2009
Fresh Cotton
online design contest

November – December 2009
Knitting against AIDS global
(see p136 – 137)

December 13th 2009
Antwerp AIDS Diner

December 2009
Global fundraiser by
rockband Tokio Hotel

UK/South Africa, 2009
VOICES documentary

Antwerp, February 2010
Party against AIDS

Antwerp, February 2010
Exhibition DAA & You

May 2010
Third edition
of Fashion against AIDS
(see p149)

From June 2010
DAA campaign
in Antwerp public transport
(see p161)

Antwerp, June 2010
Antwerp Pride
(speech, booth, concert,
flyers & condoms)
(see p160)

Antwerp, June 24th 2010
Soft opening IHAEC
(see p162 – 164)

Antwerp, June 2010
Vitrine 'Slow Fashion'
(see p174 – 175)

June 2010
'Wrap It Up Before You Fuck It
Up' T-shirts by Paul Snowden

From June 2010
Series of DAA internet ads by
Addictlab/Jan Van Mol
(see p176)

Paris, October 1st 2010
Antwerp State of Fashion

Antwerp, October 2010
Benefit auction
Campo & Campo

Brussels, December 2010 –
June 2011
Muntpunt video projections

Antwerp, December 1st 2010
Official opening IHAEC
(see p180 – 181)

BUSINESS PARTNERS AND ORGANIZATIONS WHO SUPPORT THE WORK OF DESIGNERS AGAINST AIDS

H&M, UNFPA, Y-Peer, UNAIDS, UNESCO, Dominique Models, Belspeed, Umbro, Premium, Bread & Butter, AIFW, Circleculture, Lombardia, Addictlab, American Apparel, Antwerp Pride, Inter-European Parliamentary Forum on Population and Development, Fish & Chips, Cheek Magazine, Bozar, Six Scents, Global Detox, Mistral, Fresh Cotton, Antwerp AIDS Diner, Timmermans, Sensoa, Plateforme Prévention SIDA, Lee Cooper, L'Oréal Professional, Playboy Design, The Global Business Coalition on HIV/AIDS, Tuberculosis and Malaria, Hamadi Beauty, Sense Organics, Dawanda, MAC Cosmetics, De Invasie, Talenthouse, Universal, Bravado, Flanders Fashion Institute, Dries Van Noten , Tides Foundation, King Baudoin Foundation, Oranjefonds, Maecenata, Pas Print, Cointreau, Safe Pocket, No Kidd'n, Expose NY, Maison de Mode Lille, Pardaf, Stimuli Magazine, Nineteen74, Benicassim Festival/Fiberfib, Toolbox, Be Carbon Neutral NYC, Delvaux, Designer-Vintage, IncuFashion, Modemuseum Hasselt, Value Retail, Aids Action Europe, Love Rocks, Carobati, Campo & Campo, Het Roze Huis Antwerpen, Rainbow House Brussels, ra 13 Antwerp, Basedesign…

COLOPHON

Editors
Ninette Murk
Michael James O'Brien

Coordination
Tinneke Janssens
Candice Mai Khanh Nguyen
Zoltan Gerliczki

Authors
Alain de Botton
Ninette Murk

With special contributions by
Peter Piot
Margareta van den Bosch

Design
BaseDesign
www.basedesign.com

Printed by
Proost, Turnhout

© 2010 Ludion
and the authors
© 2010 Ludion
and the photographers

All rights reserved. No part of this publication may be reproduced or transmitted in any form or by any means, electronic or mechanical, including photocopy, recording or any other information storage and retrieval system, without prior permission in writing from the publisher.

www.ludion.be
www.beautywithoutirony.com
www.designersagainstaids.com

ISBN 978-90-5544-841-8
D/2010/6328/72